Webster's Seventh of March Speech, and the Secession Movement

Herbert Darling Foster

Contents

FOREWORD 7
WEBSTER'S SEVENTH OF MARCH SPEECH AND THE SECESSION
    MOVEMENT, 1850 10
I. 12
II. 25
III. 28
IV. 31
NOTES 38

WEBSTER'S SEVENTH OF MARCH SPEECH, AND THE SECESSION MOVEMENT

BY
Herbert Darling Foster

FOREWORD

It is very curious that much of the history of the United States in the Forties and Fifties of the last century has vanished from the general memory. When a skilled historian reopens the study of Webster's "Seventh of March speech" it is more than likely that nine out of ten Americans will have to cudgel their wits endeavoring to make quite sure just where among our political adventures that famous oration fits in. How many of us could pass a satisfactory examination on the antecedent train of events--the introduction in Congress of that Wilmot Proviso designed to make free soil of all the territory to be acquired in the Mexican War; the instant and bitter reaction of the South; the various demands for some sort of partition of the conquered area between the sections, between slave labor and free labor; the unforeseen intrusion of the gold seekers of California in 1849, and their unauthorized formation of a new state based on free labor; the flaming up of Southern alarm, due not to one cause but to many, chiefly to the obvious fact that the free states were acquiring preponderance in Congress; the southern threats of secession; the fury of the Abolitionists demanding no concessions to the South, come what might; and then, just when a rupture seemed inevitable, when Northern extremists and Southern extremists seemed about to snatch control of their sections, Webster's bold play to the moderates on both sides, his scheme of compromise, announced in that famous speech on the seventh of March, 1850?

Most people are still aware that Webster was harshly criticized for making that speech. It is dimly remembered that the Abolitionists called him "Traitor", refusing to attribute to him any motive except the gaining of Southern support which might land him in the Presidency. At the time--so bitter was factional suspicion!--this view gained many adherents. It has not lost them all, even now.

This false interpretation of Webster turns on two questions--was there a real danger of secession in 1850? Was Webster sincere in deriving his policy from a sense of national peril, not from self-interest? In the study which follows Professor Foster makes an adequate case for Webster, answering the latter question. The former he deals with in a general way establishing two things, the fact of Southern readiness to secede, the attendant fact that the South changed its attitude after the Seventh of March. His limits prevent his going on to weigh and appraise the sincerity of those fanatics who so furiously maligned Webster, who created the tradition that he had cynically sold out to the Southerners. Did they believe their own fiction? The question is a large one and involves this other, did they know what was going on in the South? Did they realize that the Union on March 6, 1850, was actually at a parting of the ways,--that destruction or Civil War formed an imminent issue?

Many of those who condemned compromise may be absolved from the charge of insincerity on the ground that they did not care whether the Union was preserved or riot. Your true blue Abolitionist was very little of a materialist. Nor did he have primarily a crusading interest in the condition of the blacks. He was introspective. He wanted the responsibility for slavery taken off his own soul. As later events were to prove, he was also pretty nearly a pacifist; war for the Union, pure and simple, made no appeal to him. It was part of Webster's insight that he divined this, that he saw there was more pacifism than natural ardor in the North of 1850, saw that the precipitation of a war issue might spell the end of the United Republic. Therefore, it was to circumvent the Northern pacifists quite as much as to undermine the Southern expansionists that he offered compromise and avoided war.

But what of those other detractors of Webster, those who were for the Union and yet believed he had sold out? Their one slim defense is the conviction that the South did not mean what it said, that Webster, had he dared offend the South, could have saved the day--from their point of view--without making concessions. Professor Foster, always ready to do scrupulous justice, points out the dense ignorance in each section of the other, and there lets the matter rest. But what shall we say of a frame of mind, which in that moment of crisis, either did not read the Southern newspapers, or reading them and finding that the whole South was netted over by a systematically organized secession propaganda made no attempt to gauge its strength, scoffed at it all as buncombe! Even later historians have done the same thing. In too many cases they have assumed that because the compromise was followed by an apparent collapse of the secession propaganda, the propaganda all along was without reality. We know today that the propaganda did not collapse. For strategic reasons it changed its policy. But it went on steadily growing and gaining ground until it triumphed in 1861. Webster, not his foolish opponents, gauged its strength correctly in 1850. The clew to what actually happened in 1850 lies in the course of such an ardent Southerner as, for example, Langdon Cheeves. Early in the year, he was a leading secessionist, but at the close of the year a leading anti-secessionist. His change of front, forced upon him by his own thinking about the situation was a bitter disappointment to himself. What animated him was a deep desire to take the whole South out of the Union. When, at the opening of the year, the North seemed unwilling to compromise, he, and many another, thought their time had come. At the first Nashville Convention he advised a general secession, assuming that Virginia, "our premier state," would lead the movement and when Virginia later in the year swung over from secession to anti-secession, Cheeves reluctantly changed his policy. The compromise had not altered his views--broadly speaking it had not satisfied the Lower South--but it had done something still more eventful, it had so affected the Upper South that a united secession became for a while impossible. Therefore, Cheeves and all like him--and they were the determining factor of the hour--resolved to bide their time, to wait until their propaganda had done its work, until the entire South should agree to go out together. Their argument, all preserved in print, but ignored by historians for sixty years thereafter, was perfectly frank. As one of them put it, in the face of the changed attitude of Virginia, "to secede now would be to secede from the South."

Here is the aspect of Webster's great stroke that was so long ignored. He did not satisfy the whole South. He did not make friends for himself of Southerners generally. What he did do was to drive a wedge into the South, to divide it temporarily against itself. He arrayed the Upper South against the Lower and thus because of the ultimate purposes of men like Cheeves, with their ambition to weld the South into a genuine unit, he forced them all to stand still, and thus to give Northern pacifism a chance to ebb, Northern nationalism a chance to develop. A comprehensive brief for the defense on this crucial point in the interpretation of American history, is Professor Foster's contribution.

NATHANIEL WRIGHT STEPHENSON

WEBSTER'S SEVENTH OF MARCH SPEECH AND THE SECESSION MOVEMENT, 1850

The moral earnestness and literary skill of Whittier, Lowell, Garrison, Phillips, and Parker, have fixed in many minds the antislavery doctrine that Webster's 7th of March speech was "scandalous, treachery", and Webster a man of little or no "moral sense", courage, or statesmanship. That bitter atmosphere, reproduced by Parton and von Holst, was perpetuated a generation later by Lodge. [1]

Since 1900, over fifty publications throwing light on Webster and the Secession movement of 1850 have appeared, nearly a score containing fresh contemporary evidence. These twentieth-century historians--Garrison of Texas, Smith of Williams, Stephenson of Charleston and Yale, Van Tyne, Phillips, Fisher in his True Daniel Webster, or Ames, Hearon, and Cole in their monographs on Southern conditions--many of them born in one section and educated in another, brought into broadening relations with Northern and Southern investigators, trained in the modern historical spirit and freed by the mere lapse of time from much of the passion of slavery and civil war, have written with less emotion and more knowledge than the abolitionists, secessionists, or their disciples who preceded Rhodes.

Under the auspices of the American Historical Association have appeared the correspondence of Calhoun, of Chase, of Toombs, Stephens, and Cobb, and of Hunter of Virginia. Van Tyne's Letters of Webster (1902), including hundreds hitherto unpublished, was further supplemented in the sixteenth volume of the "National Edition" of Webster's Writings and Speeches (1903). These two editions contain, for 1850 alone, 57 inedited letters.

Manuscript collections and newspapers, comparatively unknown to earlier writers, have been utilized in monographs dealing with the situation in 1850 in

South Carolina, Mississippi, Georgia, Alabama, North Carolina, Louisiana, and Tennessee, published by. universities or historical societies.

The cooler and matured judgments of men who knew Webster personally--Foote, Stephens, Wilson, Seward, and Whittier, in the last century; Hoar, Hale, Fisher, Hosmer, and Wheeler in recent years-modify their partizan political judgments of 1850. The new printed evidence is confirmed by manuscript material: 2,500 letters of the Greenough Collection available since the publication of the recent editions of Webster's letters and apparently unused by Webster's biographers; and Hundreds of still inedited Webster Papers in the New Hampshire Historical Society, and scattered in minor collections. [2] This mass of new material makes possible and desirable a re-examination of the evidence as to (1) the danger from the secession movement in 1850; (2) Webster's change in attitude toward the disunion danger in February, 1850; (3) the purpose and character of his 7th of March speech; (4) the effects of his speech and attitude upon the secession movement.

I.

During the session of Congress of 1849-1850, the peace of the Union was threatened by problems centering around slavery and the territory acquired as a result of the Mexican War: California's demand for admission with a constitution prohibiting slavery; the Wilmot Proviso excluding slavery from the rest of the Mexican acquisitions (Utah and New Mexico); the boundary dispute between Texas and New Mexico; the abolition of slave trade in the District of Columbia; and an effective fugitive slave law to replace that of 1793.

The evidence for the steadily growing danger of secession until March, 1850, is no longer to be sought in Congressional speeches, but rather in the private letters of those men, Northern and Southern, who were the shrewdest political advisers of the South, and in the official acts of representative bodies of Southerners in local or state meetings, state legislatures, and the Nashville Convention. Even after the compromise was accepted in the South and the secessionists defeated in 1850-1851, the Southern states generally adopted the Georgia platform or its equivalent declaring that the Wilmot Proviso or the repeal of the fugitive-slave law would lead the South to "resist even (as a last resort) to a disruption of every tie which binds her to the Union". Southern disunion sentiment was not sporadic or a party matter; it was endemic.

The disunion sentiment in the North was not general; but Garrison, publicly proclaiming "I am an abolitionist and therefore for the dissolution of the Union", and his followers who pronounced "the Constitution a covenant with death and an agreement with hell", exercised a twofold effect far in excess of their numbers. In the North, abolitionists aroused bitter antagonism to slavery; in the South they strengthened the conviction of the lawfulness of slavery and the desirability of secession in preference to abolition. "The abolition question must soon divide us", a

South Carolinian wrote his former principal in Vermont. "We are beginning to look upon it [disunion] as a relief from incessant insult. I have been myself surprised at the unusual prevalence and depth of this feeling." [3] "The abolition movement", as Houston has pointed out, "prevented any considerable abatement of feeling, and added volume to the current which was to sweep the State out of the Union in 1860." [4] South Carolina's ex-governor, Hammond, wrote Calhoun in December, 1849, "the conduct of the abolitionists in congress is daily giving it [disunion] powerful aid". "The sooner we can get rid of it [the union] the better." [5] The conclusion of both Blair of Kentucky and Winthrop [6] of Massachusetts, that "Calhoun and his instruments are really solicitous to break up the Union", was warranted by Calhoun's own statement.

Calhoun, desiring to save the Union if he could, but at all events to save the South, and convinced that there was "no time to lose", hoped "a decisive issue will be made with the North". In February, 1850, he wrote, "Disunion is the only alternative that is left us." [7] At last supported by some sort of action in thirteen Southern states, and in nine states by appointment of delegates to his Southern Convention, he declared in the Senate, March 4, "the South, is united against the Wilmot proviso, and has committed itself, by solemn resolutions, to resist should it be adopted". "The South will be forced to choose between abolition and secession." "The Southern States... cannot remain, as things now are, consistently with honor and safety, in the Union." [8]

That Beverley Tucker rightly judged that this speech of Calhoun expressed what was "in the mind of every man in the State" is confirmed by the approval of Hammond and other observers; by their judgment that "everyone was ripe for disunion and no one ready to make a speech in favor of the union"; by the testimony of the governor, that South Carolina "is ready and anxious for an immediate separation"; and by the concurrent testimony of even the few "Unionists" like Petigru and Lieber, who wrote Webster, "almost everyone is for southern separation", "disunion is the... predominant sentiment". "For arming the state $350,000 has been put at the disposal of the governor." "Had I convened the legislature two or three weeks before the regular meeting," adds the governor, "such was the excited state of the public mind at that time, I am convinced South Carolina would not now have been a member of the Union. The people are very far ahead of their leaders."

Ample first-hand evidence of South Carolina's determination to secede in 1850 may be found in the Correspondence of Calhoun, in Claiborne's Quitman, in the acts of the assembly, in the newspapers, in the legislature's vote "to resist at any and all hazards", and in the choice of resistance-men to the Nashville Convention and the state convention. This has been so convincingly set forth in Ames's Calhoun and the Secession Movement of 1850, and in Hamer's Secession Movement in South Carolina, 1847-1852, that there is need of very few further illustrations. [9]

That South Carolina postponed secession for ten years was due to the Compromise. Alabama and Virginia adopted resolutions accepting the compromise in 1850-1851; and the Virginia legislature tactfully urged South Carolina to abandon secession. The 1851 elections in Alabama, Georgia, and Mississippi showed the South ready to accept the Compromise, the crucial test being in Mississippi, where the voters followed Webster's supporter, Foote. [10] That Petigru was right in maintaining that South, Carolina merely abandoned immediate and separate secession is shown by the almost unanimous vote of the South Carolina State Convention of 1852, [11] that the state was amply justified "in dissolving at once all political connection with her co-States", but refrained from this "manifest right of self-government from considerations of expediency only". [12]

In Mississippi, a preliminary convention, instigated by Calhoun, recommended the holding of a Southern convention at Nashville in June, 1850, to "adopt some mode of resistance". The "Resolutions" declared the Wilmot Proviso "such a breach of the federal compact as... will make it the duty... of the slave-holding states to treat the non-slave-holding states as enemies". The "Address" recommended "all the assailed states to provide in the last resort for their separate welfare by the formation of a compact and a Union". "The object of this [Nashville Convention] is to familiarize the public mind with the idea of dissolution", rightly judged the Richmond Whig and the Lynchburg Virginian.

Radical resistance men controlled the legislature and "cordially approved" the disunion resolution and address, chose delegates to the Nashville Convention, appropriated $20,000 for their expenses and $200,000 for "necessary measures for protecting the state... in the event of the passage of the Wilmot Proviso", etc. [13] These actions of Mississippi's legislature one day before Webster's 7th of March speech mark approximately the peak of the secession movement.

Governor Quitman, in response to public demand, called the legislature and proposed "to recommend the calling of a regular convention... with full power to annul the federal compact". "Having no hope of an effectual remedy... but in separation from the Northern States, my views of state action will look to secession." [14] The legislature supported Quitman's and Jefferson Davis's plans for resistance, censured Foote's support of the Compromise, and provided for a state convention of delegates. [15]

Even the Mississippi "Unionists" adopted the six standard points generally accepted in the South which would justify resistance. "And this is the Union party", was the significant comment of the New York Tribune. This Union Convention, however, believed that Quitman's message was treasonable and that there was ample evidence of a plot to dissolve the Union and form a Southern confederacy. Their programme was adopted by the State Convention the following year. [16] The radical Mississippians reiterated Calhoun's constitutional guarantees of sectional equality and non-interference with slavery, and declared for a Southern convention with power to recommend "secession from the Union and the formation of a Southern confederacy". [17]

"The people of Mississippi seemed... determined to defend their equality in the Union, or to retire from it by peaceful secession. Had the issue been pressed at the moment when the excitement was at its highest point, an isolated and very serious movement might have occurred, which South Carolina, without doubt, would have promptly responded to." [18]

In Georgia, evidence as to "which way the wind blows" was received by the Congressional trio, Alexander Stephens, Toombs, and Cobb, from trusted observers at home. "The only safety of the South from abolition universal is to be found in an early dissolution of the Union." Only one democrat was found justifying Cobb's opposition to Calhoun and the Southern Convention. [19]

Stephens himself, anxious to "stick to the Constitutional Union" reveals in confidential letters to Southern Unionists the rapidly growing danger of disunion. "The feeling among the Southern members for a dissolution of the Union... is becoming much more general." "Men are now [December, 1849] beginning to talk of it seriously who twelve months ago hardly permitted themselves to think of it." "Civil war in this country better be prevented if it can be." After a month's "farther and broader view", he concluded, "the crisis is not far ahead... a dismemberment of this Republic I now consider inevitable." [20]

On February 8, 1850, the Georgia legislature appropriated $30,000 for a state convention to consider measures of redress, and gave warning that anti-slavery aggressions would "induce us to contemplate the possibility of a dissolution". [21] "I see no prospect of a continuance of this Union long", wrote Stephens two days later. [22]

Speaker Cobb's advisers warned him that "the predominant feeling of Georgia" was "equality or disunion", and that "the destructives" were trying to drive the South into disunion. "But for your influence, Georgia would have been more rampant for dissolution than South Carolina ever was." "S. Carolina will secede, but we can and must put a stop to it in Georgia." [23]

Public opinion in Georgia, which had been "almost ready for immediate secession", was reversed only after the passage of the Compromise and by means of a strenuous campaign against the Secessionists which Stephens, Toombs, and Cobb were obliged to return to Georgia to conduct to a Successful issue. [24] Yet even the Unionist Convention of Georgia, elected by this campaign, voted almost unanimously "the Georgia platform" already described, of resistance, even to disruption, against the Wilmot Proviso, the repeal of the fugitive slave law, and the other measures generally selected for reprobation in the South. [25] "Even the existence of the Union depended upon the settlement"; "we would have resisted by our arms if the wrong [Wilmot Proviso] had been perpetuated", were Stephens's later judgments. [26] It is to be remembered that the Union victory in Georgia was based upon the Compromise and that Webster's share in "strengthening the friends of the Union" was recognized by Stephens.

The disunion movement manifested also dangerous strength in Virginia and Alabama, and showed possibilities of great danger in Tennessee, North Carolina, Florida, Louisiana, Maryland, Missouri, Texas, and Arkansas. The majority of the people may not have favored secession in 1850 any more than in 1860; but the leaders could and did carry most of the Southern legislatures in favor of uniting for resistance.

The "ultras" in Virginia, under the lead of Tucker, and in Alabama under Yancey, frankly avowed their desire to stimulate impossible demands so that disunion would be inevitable. Tucker at Nashville "ridiculed Webster's assertion that the Union could not be dissolved without bloodshed". On the eve of Webster's speech, Garnett of Virginia published a frank advocacy of a Southern Confederacy, repeatedly reprinted, which Clay declared "the most dangerous pamphlet he had ever read". [27] Virginia, in providing for delegates to the Nashville Convention, announced her readiness to join her "sister slave states" for "mutual defence". She later acquiesced in the Compromise, but reasserted that anti-slavery aggressions would "defeat restoration of peaceful sentiments". [28]

In Texas there was acute danger of collision over the New Mexico boundary with Federal troops which President Taylor was preparing to send. Stephens frankly repeated Quitman's threats of Southern armed support of Texas. [29] Cobb, Henderson of Texas, Duval of Kentucky, Anderson of Tennessee, and Goode of Virginia expressed similar views as to the "imminent cause of danger to the Union from Texas". The collision was avoided because the more statesmanlike attitude of Webster prevailed rather than the "soldier's" policy of Taylor.

The border states held a critical position in 1850, as they did in 1860. "If they go for the Southern movement we shall have disunion." "Everything is to depend from this day on the course of Kentucky, Tennessee and Missouri." [30] Webster's conciliatory Union policy, in harmony with that of border state leaders, like Bell of Tennessee, Benton of Missouri, Clay and Crittenden of Kentucky, enabled Maryland, Kentucky, and Missouri to stand by the Union and refuse to send delegates to the Nashville Convention.

The attitude of the Southern states toward disunion may be followed closely in their action as to the Nashville Convention. Nine Southern states approved the Convention and appointed delegates before June, 1850, six during the critical month preceding Webster's speech: Georgia, February 6, 8; Texas and Tennessee, February 11; Virginia, February 12; Alabama, just before the adjournment of the legislature, February 13; Mississippi, March 5, 6. [31] Every one of the nine seceded in 1860-1861; the border states (Maryland, Kentucky, Missouri) which kept out of the Convention in 1850 likewise kept out of secession in 1861; and only two states which seceded in 1861 failed to join the Southern movement in 1850 (North Carolina and Louisiana). This significant parallel between the action of the Southern states in 1850 and in 1860 suggests the permanent strength of the secession movement of 1850. Moreover, the alignment of leaders was strikingly the same in 1850 and 1860. Those who headed the secession movement in 1850 in their respective states were among the leaders of secession in 1860 and 1861: Rhett in South Carolina; Yancey in Alabama; Jefferson Davis and Brown in Mississippi Garnett, Goode, and Hunter in Virginia; Johnston in Arkansas; Clingman in North Carolina. On the other hand, nearly all the men who in 1850 favored the Compromise, in 1860 either remained Union men, like Crittenden, Houston of Texas, Sharkey, Lieber, Petigru, and Provost Kennedy of Baltimore, or, like Stephens, Morehead, and Foote, vainly tried to restrain secession.

In the states unrepresented at the Nashville Convention-Missouri, Kentucky, Maryland, North Carolina, and Louisiana--there was much sympathy with the Southern movement. In Louisiana, the governor's proposal to send delegates was blocked by the Whigs. [32] "Missouri", in case of the Wilmot Proviso, "will be found in hearty co-operation with the slave-holding states for mutual protection against... Northern fanaticism", her legislature resolved. [33] Missouri's instructions to her senators were denounced as "disunion in their object" by her own Senator Benton. The Maryland legislature resolved, February 26: "Maryland will take her position with her Southern sister states in the maintenance of the constitution with all its compromises." The Whig senate, however, prevented sanctioning of the convention and sending of delegates. Florida's governor wrote the governor of South Carolina that Florida would co-operate with Virginia and South Carolina "in any measure in defense of our common Constitution and sovereign dignity". "Florida has resolved to resist to the extent of revolution", declared her representative in Congress, March 5. Though the Whigs did not support the movement, five delegates came from Florida to the Nashville Convention. [34]

In Kentucky, Crittenden's repeated messages against "disunion" and "entangling engagements" reveal the danger seen by a Southern Union governor. [35] Crittenden's changing attitude reveals the growing peril, and the growing reliance on Webster's and Clay's plans. By April, Crittenden recognized that "the Union is endangered", "the case... rises above ordinary rules", "circumstances have rather changed". He reluctantly swung from Taylor's plan of dealing with California alone, to the Clay and Webster idea of settling the "whole controversy". [36] Representative Morehead wrote Crittenden, "The extreme Southern gentlemen would secretly deplore the settlement of this question. The magnificence of a Southern Confederacy... is a dazzling allurement." Clay like Webster, saw "the alternative, civil war". [37]

In North Carolina, the majority appear to have been loyal to the Union; but the extremists--typified by Clingman, the public meeting at Wilmington, and the newspapers like the Wilmington Courier--reveal the presence of a dangerously aggressive body "with a settled determination to dissolve the Union" and frankly "calculating the advantages of a Southern Confederacy." Southern observers in this state reported that "the repeal of the Fugitive Slave Law or the abolition of slavery in the District will dissolve the Union". The North Carolina legislature acquiesced in the Compromise but counselled retaliation in case of anti-slavery aggressions. [38] Before the assembling of the Southern convention in June, every one of the Southern states, save Kentucky, had given some encouragement to the Southern movement, and Kentucky had given warning and proposed a compromise through Clay. [39]

Nine Southern states-Virginia, South Carolina, Georgia, Alabama, Mississippi, Texas, Arkansas, Florida, and Tennessee sent about 176 delegates to the Nashville Convention. The comparatively harmless outcome of this convention, in June, led earlier historians to underestimate the danger of the resistance movement in February and March when backed by legislatures, newspapers, and public opinion, before the effect was felt of the death of Calhoun and Taylor, and of Webster's support of conciliation. Stephens and the Southern Unionists rightly recognized that the Nashville Convention "will be the nucleus of another sectional assembly". "A fixed alienation of feeling will be the result." "The game of the destructives is to use the Missouri Compromise principle [as demanded by the Nashville Convention] as a medium of defeating all adjustments and then to... infuriate the South and drive her into measures that must end in disunion." "All who go to the Nashville Convention are ultimately to fall into that position." This view is confirmed by Judge Warner and other observers in Georgia and by the unpublished letters of Tucker. [40] "Let the Nashville Convention be held", said the Columbus, Georgia, Sentinel, "and let the undivided voice of the South go forth... declaring our determination to resist even to civil war." [41] The speech of Rhett of South Carolina, author of the convention's "Address", "frankly and boldly unfurled the flag of disunion". "If every

Southern State should quail... South Carolina alone should make the issue." "The opinion of the [Nashville] address is, and I believe the opinion of a large portion of the Southern people is, that the Union cannot be made to endure", was delegate Barnwell's admission to Webster. [42]

The influence of the Compromise is brought out in the striking change in the attitude of Senator Foote, and of judge Sharkey of Mississippi, the author of the radical "Address" of the preliminary Mississippi Convention, and chairman of both this and the Nashville Convention. After the Compromise measures were reported in May by Clay and Webster's committee, Sharkey became convinced that the Compromise should be accepted and so advised Foote. Sharkey also visited Washington and helped to pacify the rising storm by "suggestions to individual Congressmen". [43] In the Nashville Convention, Sharkey therefore exercised a moderating influence as chairman and refused to sign its disunion address. Convinced that the Compromise met essential Southern demands, Sharkey urged that "to resist it would be to dismember the Union". He therefore refused to call a second meeting of the Nashville Convention. For this change in position he was bitterly criticized by Jefferson Davis. [44] Foote recognized the "emergency" at the same time that Webster did, and on February 25, proposed his committee of thirteen to report some "scheme of compromise". Parting company with Calhoun, March 5, on the thesis that the South could not safely remain without new "constitutional guarantees", Foote regarded Webster's speech as "unanswerable", and in April came to an understanding with him as to Foote's committee and their common desire for prompt consideration of California. The importance of Foote's influence in turning the tide in Mississippi, through his pugnacious election campaign, and the significance of his judgment of the influence of Webster and his speech have been somewhat overlooked, partly perhaps because of Foote's swashbuckling characteristics. [45]

That the Southern convention movement proved comparatively innocuous in June is due in part to confidence inspired by the conciliatory policy of one outstanding Northerner, Webster. "Webster's speech", said Winthrop, "has knocked the Nashville Convention into a cocked hat." [46] "The Nashville Convention has been blown by your giant effort to the four winds." [47] "Had you spoken out before this, I verily believe the Nashville Convention had not been thought of. Your speech has disarmed and quieted the South." [48] Webster's speech caused hesitation in the

South. "This has given courage to all who wavered in their resolution or who were secretly opposed to the measure [Nashville Convention]." [49]

Ames cites nearly a store of issues of newspapers in Mississippi, South Carolina, Louisiana, North Carolina, Georgia, and Virginia reflecting the change in public opinion in March. Even some of the radical papers referred to the favorable effect of Webster's speech and "spirit" in checking excitement. "The Jackson (Mississippi) Southron had at first supported the movement [for a Southern Convention], but by March it had grown lukewarm and before the Convention assembled, decidedly opposed it. The last of May it said, 'not a Whig paper in the State approves'." In the latter part of March, not more than a quarter of sixty papers from ten slave-holding states took decided ground for a Southern Convention. [50] The Mississippi Free Trader tried to check the growing support of the Compromise, by claiming that Webster's speech lacked Northern backing. A South Carolina pamphlet cited the Massachusetts opposition to Webster as proof of the political strength of abolition. [51]

The newer, day by day, first-hand evidence, in print and manuscript, shows the Union in serious danger, with the culmination during the three weeks preceding Webster's speech; with a moderation during March; a growing readiness during the summer to await Congressional action; and slow, acquiescence in the Compromise measures of September, but with frank assertion on the part of various Southern states of the right and duty of resistance if the compromise measures were violated. Even in December, 1850, Dr. Alexander of Princeton found sober Virginians fearful that repeal of the Fugitive Slave Act would throw Virginia info the Southern movement and that South Carolina "by some rash act" would precipitate "the crisis". "All seem to regard bloodshed as the inevitable result." [52]

To the judgments and legislative acts of Southerners already quoted, may be added some of the opinions of men from the North. Erving, the diplomat, wrote from New York, "The real danger is in the fanatics and disunionists of the North". "I see no salvation but in the total abandonment of the Wilmot Proviso." Edward Everett, on the contrary, felt that "unless some southern men of influence have courage enough to take grounds against the extension of slavery and in favor of abolition... we shall infallibly separate". [53]

A Philadelphia editor who went to Washington to learn the real sentiments of the Southern members, reported February 1, that if the Wilmot Proviso were not given up, ample provision made for fugitive slaves and avoidance of interference with slavery in the District of Columbia, the South would secede, though this was not generally believed in the North. "The North must decide whether she would have the Wilmot Proviso without the Union or the Union without the Wilmot Proviso." [54]

In answer to inquiries from the Massachusetts legislature as to whether the Southern attitude was "bluster" or "firm Resolve", Winthrop wrote, "the country has never been in more serious exigency than at present". "The South is angry, mad." "The Union must be saved... by prudence and forbearance." "Most sober men here are apprehensive that the end of the Union is nearer than they have ever before imagined." Winthrop's own view on February 19 had been corroborated by General Scott, who wrote him four days earlier, "God preserve the Union is my daily prayer, in and out of church". [55]

Webster however, as late as February 14, believed that there was no "serious danger". February 16, he still felt that "if, on our side, we keep cool, things will come to no dangerous pass". [56] But within the next week, three acts in Washington modified Webster's optimism: the filibuster of Southern members, February 18; their triumph in conference, February 19; their interview with Taylor about February 23.

On February 18, under the leadership of Stephens, the Southern representatives mustered two-thirds of the Southern Whigs and a majority from every Southern state save Maryland for a successful series of over thirty filibustering votes against the admission of California without consideration of the question of slavery in New Mexico and Utah. So indisputable was the demonstration of Southern power to block not only the President's plan but all Congressional legislation, that the Northern leaders next day in conference with. Southern representatives agreed that California should be admitted with her free constitution, but that in New Mexico and Utah government should be organized with no prohibition of slavery and with power to form, in respect to slavery, such constitutions as the people pleased--agreements practically enacted in the Compromise. [57]

The filibuster of the 18th of February, Mann described as "a revolutionary proceeding". Its alarming effect on the members of the Cabinet was commented upon by the Boston Advertiser, February 19. The New York Tribune, February 20, recognized the determination of the South to secede unless the Missouri Compromise line were extended to the Pacific. February 22, the Springfield Republican declared that "if the Union cannot be preserved" without the extension of slavery, "we allow the tie of Union to be severed". It was on this day, that Webster decided "to make a Union speech and discharge a clear conscience".

That same week (apparently February 23) occurred the famous interview of Stephens and Toombs with Taylor which convinced the President that the Southern movement "means disunion". This was Taylor's judgment expressed to Weed and Hamlin, "ten minutes after the interview". A week later the President seemed to Horace Mann to be talking like a child about his plans to levy an embargo and blockade the Southern harbors and "save the Union". Taylor was ready to appeal to arms against "these Southern men in Congress [who] are trying to bring on civil war" in connection with the critical Texas boundary question. [58]

On this 23d of February, Greeley, converted from his earlier and characteristic optimism, wrote in his leading editorial: "instead of scouting or ridiculing as chimerical the idea of a Dissolution of the Union, we firmly believe that there are sixty members of Congress who this day desire it and are plotting to effect it. We have no doubt the Nashville Convention will be held and that the leading purpose of its authors is the separation of the slave states... with the formation of an independent Confederacy." "This plot... is formidable." He warned against "needless provocation which would supply weapons to the Disunionists". A private letter to Greeley from Washington, the same day, says: "II---- is alarmed and confident that blood will be spilt on the floor of the House. Many members go to the House armed every day. W---- is confident that Disunionism is now inevitable. He knows intimately nearly all the Southern members, is familiar with their views and sees the letters that reach them from their constituents. He says the most ultra are well backed up in their advices from home." [59]

The same February 23, the Boston Advertiser quoted the Washington correspondence of the Journal of Commerce: "excitement pervades the whole South, and Southern members say that it has gone beyond their control, that their tone is moderate in comparison with that of their people". "Persons who condemn Mr. Clay's resolutions now trust to some vague idea that Mr. Webster can do something better." "If Mr. Webster has any charm by the magic influence of which he can control the ultraism, of the North and of the South, he cannot too soon try its effects." "If Kentucky, Tennessee, Missouri go for the Southern movement, we shall have disunion and as much of war as may answer the purposes either of Northern or Southern fanaticism." On this Saturday, February 23, also, "several Southern members of Congress had a long and interesting interview with Mr. Webster". "The whole subject was discussed and the result is, that the limitations of a compromise have been examined, which are satisfactory to our Southern brethren. This is good news, and will surround Mr. Webster's position with an uncommon interest." [60]

"Webster is the only man in the Senate who has a position which would enable him to present a plan which would be carried", said Pratt of Maryland. [61] The National Intelligencer, which had hitherto maintained the safety of the Union, confessed by February 21 that "the integrity of the Union is at some hazard", quoting Southern evidence of this. On February 25, Foote, in proposing to the Senate a committee of thirteen to report some scheme of compromise, gave it as his conclusion from consultation with both houses, that unless something were done at once, power would pass from Congress.

II.

It was under these highly critical circumstances that Webster, on Sunday, February 24, the day on which he was accustomed to dine with his unusually well-informed friends, Stephens, Toombs, Clay and Hale, wrote to his only surviving son:

I am nearly broken down with labor and anxiety. I know not how to meet the present emergency, or with what weapons to beat down the Northern and Southern follies, now raging in equal extremes. If you can possibly leave home, I want you to be here, a day or two before I speak... I have poor spirits and little courage. Non sum qualis eram. [62]

Mr. Lodge's account of this critical February period shows ignorance not only of the letter of February 24, but of the real situation. He relies upon von Holst instead of the documents, then misquotes him on a point of essential chronology, and from unwarranted assumptions and erroneous and incomplete data draws unreliable conclusions. Before this letter of February 24 and the new cumulative evidence of the crisis, there falls to the ground the sneer in Mr. Lodge's question, "if [Webster's] anxiety was solely of a public nature, why did it date from March 7 when, prior to that time, there was much greater cause for alarm than afterwards?" Webster was anxious before the 7th of March, as so many others were, North and South, and his extreme anxiety appears in the letter of February 24, as well as in repeated later utterances. No one can read through the letters of Webster without recognizing that he had a genuine anxiety for the safety of the Union; and that neither in his letters nor elsewhere is there evidence that in his conscience he was "ill at ease" or "his mind not at peace". Here as elsewhere, Mr. Lodge's biography, written over forty years ago, reproduces anti-slavery bitterness and ignorance of facts (pardonable in 1850) and seriously misrepresents Webster's character and the situation in that year. [63]

By the last week in February and the first in March, the peak of the secession movement was reached. Never an alarmist, Webster, like others who loved the Union, become convinced during this critical last week in February of an "emergency". He determined "to make a Union Speech and discharge a clear conscience." "I made up my mind to risk myself on a proposition for a general pacification. I resolved to push my skiff from the shore alone." "We are in a crisis," he wrote June 2, "if conciliation makes no progress." "It is a great emergency, a great exigency, that the country is placed in", he said in the Senate, June 17. "We have," he wrote in October, "gone through the most important crisis which has occurred since the foundation of the government." A year later he added at Buffalo, "if we had not settled these agitating questions [by the Compromise]... in my opinion, there would have been civil war". In Virginia, where he had known the situation even better, he declared, "I believed in my conscience that a crisis was at hand, a dangerous, a fearful crisis." [64]

Rhodes's conclusion that there was "little danger of an overt act of secession while General Taylor was in the presidential chair" was based on evidence then incomplete and is abandoned by more recent historians. It is moreover significant that, of the speeches cited by Rhodes, ridiculing the danger of secession, not one was delivered before Webster's speech. All were uttered after the danger had been lessened by the speeches and attitude of Clay and Webster. Even such Northern anti-slavery speeches illustrated danger of another sort. Hale of New Hampshire "would let them go" rather than surrender the rights threatened by the fugitive slave bill. [65] Giddings in the very speech ridiculing the danger of disunion said, "when they see fit to leave the Union, I would say to them 'Go in peace'". [66] Such utterances played into the hands of secessionists, strengthening their convictions that the North despised the South and would not fight to keep her in the Union.

It is now clear that in 1850 as in 1860 the average Northern senator or anti-slavery minister or poet was ill-informed or careless as to the danger of secession, and that Webster and the Southern Unionists were well-informed and rightly anxious. Theodore Parker illustrated the bitterness that befogs the mind. He concluded that there was no danger of dissolution because "the public funds of the United States did not go down one mill." The stock market might, of course, change from many causes, but Parker was wrong as to the facts. An examination of the daily sales of United States bonds in New York, 1849-1850, shows that the change, instead of being, "not one mill," as Parker asserted, was four or five dollars during this period; and what change there was, was downward before Webster's speech and upward thereafter. [67]

We now realize what Webster knew and feared in 1849-1850. "If this strife between the South and the North goes on, we shall have war, and who is ready for that?" "There would have been a Civil War if the Compromise had not passed." The evidence confirms Thurlow Weed's mature judgment: "the country had every appearance of being on the eve of a Revolution." [68] On February 28, Everett recognized that "the radicals at the South have made up their minds to separate, the catastrophe seems to be inevitable". [69]

On March 1, Webster recorded his determination "to make an honest, truth-telling speech, and a Union speech" [691] The Washington correspondent of the Advertiser, March 4, reported that Webster will "take a large view of the state of things and advocate a straightforward course of legislation essentially such as the President has recommended". "To this point public sentiment has been gradually converging." "It will tend greatly to confirm opinion in favor of this course should it meet with the decided concurrence of Mr. Webster." The attitude of the plain citizen is expressed by Barker, of Beaver, Pennsylvania, on the same day: "do it, Mr. Webster, as you can, do it as a bold and gifted statesman and patriot; reconcile the North and South and PRESERVE the UNION". "Offer, Mr. Webster, a liberal compromise to the South." On March 4 and 5, Calhoun's Senate speech reasserted that the South, no longer safe in the Union, possessed the right of peaceable secession. On the 6th of March, Webster went over the proposed speech of the next morning with his son, Fletcher, Edward Curtis, and Peter Harvey. [70]

III.

It was under the cumulative stress of such convincing evidence, public and private utterances, and acts in Southern legislatures and in Congress, that Webster made his Union speech on the 7th of March. The purpose and character of the speech are rightly indicated by its title, "The Constitution and the Union", and by the significant dedication to the people of Massachusetts: "Necessity compels me to speak true rather than pleasing things." "I should indeed like to please you; but I prefer to save you, whatever be your attitude toward me." [71] The malignant charge that this speech was "a bid for the presidency" was long ago discarded, even by Lodge. It unfortunately survives in text-books more concerned with "atmosphere" than with truth. The modern investigator finds no evidence for it and every evidence against it. Webster was both too proud and too familiar with the political situation, North and South, to make such a monstrous mistake. The printed or manuscript letters to or from Webster in 1850 and 1851 show him and his friends deeply concerned over the danger to the Union, but not about the presidency. There is rarest mention of the matter in letters by personal or political friends; none by Webster, so far as the writer has observed.

If one comes to the speech familiar with both the situation in 1850 as now known, and with Webster's earlier and later speeches and private letters, one finds his position and arguments on the 7th of March in harmony with his attitude toward Union and slavery, and with the law and the facts. Frankly reiterating both his earlier view of slavery "as a great moral, political and social evil" and his lifelong devotion to the Union and its constitutional obligations, Webster took national, practical, courageous grounds. On the fugitive slave bill and the Wilmot Proviso, where cautious Whigs like Winthrop and Everett were inclined to keep quiet in view of Northern popular feeling, Webster "took a large view of things" and resolved, as Foote saw, to risk his reputation in advocating the only practicable solution. Not only was Webster thoroughly familiar with the facts, but he was pre-eminently logical and, as Calhoun had admitted, once convinced, "he cannot look truth in the face and oppose it by arguments". [72] He therefore boldly faced the truth that the Wilmot Proviso (as it proved later) was needless, and would irritate Southern Union men and play into hands of disunionists who frankly desired to exploit this "insult" to excite secession sentiment. In a like case ten years later, "the Republican party took precisely the same ground held by Mr. Webster in 1850 and acted from the motives that inspired the 7th of March speech". [73]

Webster's anxiety for a conciliatory settlement of the highly dangerous Texas boundary situation (which incidentally narrowed slave territory) was as consistent with his national Union policy, as his desires for California's admission as a free state and for prohibition of the slave-trade in the District of Columbia were in accord with his opposition to slavery. Seeing both abolitionists and secessionists threatening the Union, he rebuked both severely for disloyalty to their "constitutional obligations", while he pleaded for a more conciliatory attitude, for faith and charity rather than "heated imaginations". The only logical alternative to the union policy was disunion, advocated alike by Garrisonian abolitionists and Southern secessionists. "The Union... was thought to be in danger, and devotion to the Union rightfully inclined men to yield... where nothing else could have so inclined them", was Lincoln's luminous defense of the Compromise in his debate with Douglas. [74]

Webster's support of the constitutional provision for "return of persons held to service" was not merely that of a lawyer. It was in accord with a deep and statesmanlike conviction that "obedience to established government... is a Christian duty", the seat of law is "the bosom of God, her voice the harmony of the universe". [75] Offensive as this law was to the North, the only logical alternatives were to fulfil or to annul the Constitution. Webster chose to risk his reputation; the extreme abolitionists, to risk the Union. Webster felt, as his opponents later recognized, that "the habitual cherishing of the principle", "resistance to unjust laws is obedience to God", threatened the Constitution. "He... addressed himself, therefore, to the duty of calling the American people back from revolutionary theories to... submission to authority." [76] As in 1830 against Haynes, so in 1850 against Calhoun and disunion, Webster stood not as "a Massachusetts man, but as an American", for "the preservation of the Union". [77] In both speeches he held that he was acting not for Massachusetts, but for the "whole country" (1830), "the good of the whole" (1850). His devotion to the Union and his intellectual balance led him to reject the impatience, bitterness, and disunion sentiments of abolitionists and secessionists, and to work on longer lines. "We must wait for the slow progress of moral causes", a doctrine already announced in 1840, he reiterated in 1850,--"the effect of moral causes, though sure is slow." [78]

IV.

The earlier accounts of Webster's losing his friends as a result of his speech are at variance with the facts. Cautious Northerners naturally hesitated to support him and face both the popular convictions on fugitive slaves and the rasping vituperation that exhausted sacred and profane history in the epithets current in that "era of warm journalistic manners"; Abolitionists and Free Soilers congratulated one another that they had "killed Webster". In Congress no Northern man save Ashmun of Massachusetts supported him in any speech for months. On the other hand, Webster did retain the friendship and confidence of leaders and common men North and South, and the tremendous influence of his personality and "unanswerable" arguments eventually swung the North for the Compromise. From Boston came prompt expressions of "entire concurrence" in his speech by 800 representative men, including George Ticknor, William H. Prescott, Rufus Choate, Josiah Quincy, President Sparks and Professor Felton of Harvard, Professors Woods, Stuart, and Emerson of Andover, and other leading professional, literary, and business men. Similar addresses were sent to him from about the same number of men in New York, from supporters in Newburyport, Medford, Kennebeck River, Philadelphia, the Detroit Common Council, Manchester, New Hampshire, and "the neighbors" in Salisbury. His old Boston Congressional district triumphantly elected Eliot, one of Webster's most loyal supporters, by a vote of 2,355 against 473 for Charles Sumner. [781] The Massachusetts legislature overwhelmingly defeated a proposal to instruct Webster to vote for the Wilmot Proviso. Scores of unpublished letters in the New Hampshire Historical Society and the Library of Congress reveal hearty approval from both parties and all sections. Winthrop of Massachusetts, too cautious to endorse Webster's entire position, wrote to the governor of Massachusetts that as a result of the speech, "disunion stock is already below par". [79] "You have performed the responsible duties of, a national Senator", wrote General Dearborn. "I thank you because you did not speak upon the subject as a Massachusetts man", said Reverend Thomas Worcester of Boston, an overseer of Harvard. "Your speech has saved the Union", was the verdict of Barker of Pennsylvania, a man not of Webster's party. [80] "The Union threatened... you have come to the rescue, and all disinterested lovers of that Union must rally round you", wrote Wainwright of New York. In Alabama, Reverend J. W. Allen recognized the "comprehensive and self-forgetting spirit of patriotism" in Webster, "which, if followed, would save the Union, unite the country and prevent the danger in the Nashville Convention". Like approval of Webster's "patriotic stand for the preservation of the Union" was sent from Green County and Greensboro in Alabama and from Tennessee and Virginia. [81] "The preservation of the Union is the only safety-valve. On Webster depends the tranquility of the country", says an anonymous writer from Charleston, a native of Massachusetts and former pupil of Webster. [82] Poinsett and Francis Lieber, South Carolina Unionists, expressed like views. [83] The growing influence of the speech is testified to in letters from all sections. Linus Child of Lowell finds it modifying his own previous opinions and believes that "shortly if not at this moment, it will be approved by a large majority of the people of Massachusetts". [84] "Upon sober second thought, our people will generally coincide with your views", wrote ex-Governor and ex-Mayor Armstrong of Boston. [85] "Every day adds to the number of those who agree with you", is the confirmatory testimony of Dana, trustee of Andover and former president of Dartmouth. [86] "The effect of your speech begins to be felt", wrote ex-Mayor Eliot of Boston. [87] Mayor Huntington of Salem at first felt the speech to be too Southern; but "subsequent events at North and South have entirely satisfied me that you were right... and vast numbers of others here in Massachusetts were wrong." "The change going on in me has been going on all around me." "You saw farther ahead than the rest or most of us and had the courage and patriotism to stand upon the true ground." [88] This significant inedited letter is but a specimen of the change of attitude manifested in hundreds of letters from "slow and cautious Whigs". [89] One of these, Edward Everett, unable to accept Webster's attitude on Texas and the fugitive slave bill, could not "entirely concur" in the Boston letter of approval. "I think our friend will be able to carry the weight of it at home, but as much as ever." "It would, as you justly said," he wrote Winthrop, "have ruined any other man." This probably gives the position taken at first by a good many moderate anti-slavery then. Everett's later attitude is likewise typical of a change in New England. He wrote in 1851 that Webster's speech "more than any other cause, contributed to avert the catastrophe", and was "a practical basis for the adjustment of controversies, which had already gone far to dissolve the Union". [90]

Isaac Hill, a bitter New Hampshire political opponent, confesses that Webster's "kindly answer" to Calhoun was wiser than his own might have been. Hill, an experienced political observer, had feared in the month preceding Webster's speech a "disruption of the Union" with "no chance of escaping a conflict of blood". He felt that the censures of Webster were undeserved, that Webster was not merely right, but had "power he can exercise at the North, beyond any other man", and that "all that is of value will declare in favor of the great principles of your late Union speech". "Its tranquilizing effect upon public opinion has been wonderful"; "it has almost the unanimous support of this community", wrote the New York philanthropist Minturn. "The speech made a powerful impression in this state... Men feel they can stand on it with security." [93] In Cincinnati, Baltimore, Philadelphia, New York, and Pittsfield (with only one exception) the speech was found "wise and patriotic". [94] The sender of a resolution of approval from the grand jury of the United States court at Indianapolis says that such judgment is almost universal. [95] "It is thought you may save the country... you may keep us still united", wrote Thornton of Memphis, who soberly records the feeling of thoughtful men that the Southern purpose of disunion was stronger than appeared in either newspapers or political gatherings. [96] "Your speech has disarmed-has, quieted the South; [97] has rendered invaluable service to the harmony and union of the South and the North". [98] "I am confident of the higher approbation, not of a single section of the Union, but of all sections", wrote a political opponent in Washington. [99]

The influence of Webster in checking the radical purposes of the Nashville Convention has been shown above. [100]

All classes of men from all sections show a substantial and growing backing of Webster's 7th of March speech as "the only statesmanlike and practicable way to save the Union". "To you, more than to any other statesman of modern times, do the people of this country owe their national feeling which we trust is to save this

Union in this its hour of trial", was the judgment of "the neighbors", the plain farmers of Webster's old New Hampshire home. [101] Outside of the Abolition and Free Soil press, the growing tendency in newspapers, like that of their readers, was to support Webster's logical position. [102]

Exaggerated though some of these expressions of approval may have been, they balance the exaggerated vituperation of Webster in the anti-slavery press; and the extremes of approval and disapproval both concur in recognizing the widespread effect of the speech. "No speech ever delivered in Congress produced... so beneficial a change of opinion. The change of, feeling and temperament wrought in Congress by this speech is miraculous." [103]

The contemporary testimony to Webster's checking of disunion is substantiated by the conclusions of Petigru of South Carolina, Cobb of Georgia in 1852, Allen of Pennsylvania in 1853, and by Stephens's mature judgment of "the profound sensation upon the public mind throughout the Union made by Webster's 7th of March speech. The friends of the Union under the Constitution were strengthened in their hopes and inspired with renewed energies." [104] In 1866 Foote wrote, "The speech produced beneficial effects everywhere." "His statement of facts was generally looked upon as unanswerable; his argumentative conclusions appeared to be inevitable; his conciliatory tone.. . softened the sensibilities of all patriots." [105] "He seems to have gauged more accurately [than most] the grave dangers which threatened the republic and... the fearful consequences which must follow its disruption", was Henry Wilson's later and wiser judgment. [106] "The general judgment," said Senator Hoar in 1899, "seems to be coming to the conclusion that Webster differed from the friends of freedom of his time not in a weaker moral sense, but only in a larger, and profounder prophetic vision." "He saw what no other man saw, the certainty of civil war. I was one of those who... judged him severely, but I have learned better." "I think of him now... as the orator who bound fast with indissoluble strength the bonds of union." [107]

Modern writers, North and South-Garrison, Chadwick, T. C. Smith, Merriam, for instance [108]--now recognize the menace of disunion in 1850 and the service of Webster in defending the Union. Rhodes, though condemning Webster's support of the fugitive slave bill, recognizes that the speech was one of the few that really altered public opinion and won necessary Northern support for the Compromise. "We see now that in the War of the Rebellion his principles were mightier than those of Garrison." "It was not the Liberty or Abolitionist party, but the Union party that won." [109]

Postponement of secession for ten years gave the North preponderance in population, voting power, production, and transportation; new party organization; and convictions which made man-power and economic resources effective. The Northern lead of four million people in 1850 had increased to seven millions by 1860. In 1850, each section had thirty votes in the Senate; in 1860, the North had a majority of six, due to the admission of California, Oregon, and Minnesota. In the House of Representatives, the North had added seven to her majority. The Union states and territories built during the decade 15,000 miles of railroad, to 7,000 or 8,000 in the eleven seceding states. In shipping, the North in 1860 built about 800 vessels to the seceding states' 200. In 1860, in the eleven most important industries for war, Chadwick estimates that the Union states produced $735,500,000; the seceding states $75,250,000, "a manufacturing productivity eleven times as great for the North as for the South". [110] In general, during the decade, the census figures for 1860 show that since 1850 the North had increased its man-power, transportation, and economic production from two to fifty times as fast as the South, and that in 1860 the Union states were from two to twelve times as powerful as the seceding states.

Possibly Southern secessionists and Northern abolitionists had some basis for thinking that the North would let the "erring sisters depart in peace" in 1850. Within the next ten years, however, there came a decisive change. The North, exasperated by the Kansas-Nebraska Act of 1854, the high-handed acts of Southerners in Kansas in 1856, and the Dred Scott dictum of the Supreme Court in 1857, felt that these things amounted to a repeal of the Missouri Compromise and the opening up of the territory to slavery. In 1860 Northern conviction, backed by an effective, thorough party platform on a Union basis, swept the free states. In 1850, it was a "Constitutional Union" party that accepted the Compromise and arrested secession in the South; and Webster, foreseeing a "remodelling of parties", had prophesied that "there must be a Union party". [111] Webster's spirit and speeches and his strengthening of federal power through Supreme Court cases won by his arguments had helped to furnish the conviction which underlay the Union Party of 1860 and 1964. His consistent opposition to nullification and secession, and his appeal to the

Union and to the Constitution during twenty years preceding the Civil War--from his reply to Hayne to his seventh of March speech--had developed a spirit capable of making economic and political power effective.

Men inclined to sneer at Webster for his interest in manufacturing, farming, and material prosperity, may well remember that in his mind, and more slowly in the minds of the North, economic progress went hand in hand with the development of union and of liberty secured by law.

Misunderstandings regarding both the political crisis and the personal character of the man are already disappearing as fact replaces fiction, as "truth gets a hearing", in the fine phrase of Wendell Phillips. There is nothing about Daniel Webster to be hidden. Not moral blindness but moral insight and sound political principles reveal themselves to the reader of Webster's own words in public speech and unguarded private letter. One of those great men who disdained to vindicate himself, he does not need us but we need him and his vision that Liberty comes through Union, and healing through cooperation, not through hate.

Whether we look to the material progress of the North from 1850 to 1860 or to its development in "imponderables", Webster's policy and his power over men's thoughts and deeds were essential factors in the ultimate triumph of the Union, which would have been at least dubious had secession been attempted in 1850. It was a soldier, not the modern orator, who first said that "Webster shotted our guns". A letter to Senator Hoar from another Union soldier says that he kept up his heart as he paced up and down as sentinel in an exposed place by repeating over and over, "Liberty and Union now and forever, one and inseparable". [112] Hosmer tells us that he and his boyhood friends of the North in 1861 "did not argue much the question of the right of secession", but that it was the words of Webster's speeches, "as familiar to us as the sentences of the Lord's prayer and scarcely less consecrated,... with which we sprang to battle". Those boys were not ready in 1850. The decisive human factors in the Civil War were the men bred on the profound devotion to the Union which Webster shared with others equally patriotic, but less profoundly logical, less able to mould public opinion. Webster not only saw the vision himself; he had the genius to make the plain American citizen see that liberty could come through union and not through disunion. Moreover, there was in Webster and the Compromise of 1850 a spirit of conciliation, and therefore there was on the part of the North a belief that they had given the South a "square deal", and a corresponding indignation at the attempts in the next decade to expand slavery by violating the Compromises of 1820 and 1850. So, by 1860, the decisive border states and Northwest were ready to stand behind the Union.

When Lincoln, born in a border state, coming to manhood in the Northwest, and bred on Webster's doctrine,--"the Union is paramount",--accepted for the second time the Republican nomination and platform, he summed up the issues of the war, as he had done before, in Webster's words. Lincoln, who had grown as masterly in his choice of words as he had become profound in his vision of issues, used in 1864 not the more familiar and rhetorical phrases of the reply to Hayne, but the briefer, more incisive form, "Liberty and Union", of Webster's "honest, truth-telling, Union speech" on the 7th of March, 1850. [113]

HERBERT DARLING FOSTER.

NOTES:

[1: Cf. Parton with Lodge on intellect, morals, indolence, drinking, 7th of March speech, Webster's favorite things in England; references, note 63, below.]

[2: In the preparation of this article, manuscripts have been used from the following collections: the Greenough, Hammond, and Clayton (Library of Congress); Winthrop and Appleton (Mass. Hist. Soc.); Garrison (Boston Public Library); N.H. Hist. Soc.; Dartmouth College; Middletown (Conn.) Hist. Soc.; Mrs. Alfred E. Wyman.]

[3: Bennett, Dec. 1, 1848, to Partridge, Norwich University. MS. Dartmouth.]

[4: Houston, Nullification in South Carolina, p. 141. Further evidence of Webster's thesis that abolitionists had developed Southern reaction in Phillips, South in the Building of the Nation, IV, 401-403; and unpublished letters approving Webster's speech.]

[5: Calhoun, Corr., Amer. Hist. Assoc., Annual Report (1899, vol 11.), pp. 1193-1194.]

[6: To Crittenden, Dec. 20, 1849, Smith, polit. Hist. Slavery, I. 122; Winthrop MSS., Jan. 6, 1850.]

[7: Calhoun, Corr., p. 781; cf. 764-766, 778, 780, 783-784.]

[8: Cong. Globe, XXI. 451-455, 463; Corr., p. 784. On Calhoun's attitude, Ames, Calhoun, pp. 6-7; Stephenson, in Yale Review, 1919, p. 216; Newbury in South Atlantic Quarterly, XI. 259; Hamer, Secession Movement in South Carolina, 1847-1852, pp. 49-54.]

[9: Calhoun, Corr., Amer. Hist. Assoc., Annual Report (1899, vol. II), pp. 1210-1212; Toombs, Corr., (id., 1911, vol. II), pp. 188, 217; Coleman, Crittenden, I. 363; Hamer, pp. 55-56, 46-48, 54, 82-83; Ames, Calhoun, pp. 21-22, 29; Claiborne, Quitman, H. 36-39.]

[10: Hearon, Miss. and the Compromise of 1850, p. 209.]

[11: A letter to Webster, Oct. 22, 1851, Greenough MSS., shows the strength of Calhoun's secession ideas. Hamer, p. 125, quotes part.]

[12: Hamer, p. 142; Hearon, p. 220.]

[13: Mar. 6, 1850. Laws (Miss.), pp. 521-526.]

[14: Claiborne, Quitman, IL 37; Hearon, p. 161 n.]

[15: Hearon, pp. 180-181; Claiborne, Quitman, II. 51-52.]

[16: Nov. 10, 1850, Hearon, pp. 178-180; 1851, pp. 209-212.]

[17: Dec. 10, Southern Rights Assoc. Hearon, pp. 183-187.]

[18: Claiborne, Quitman, II. 52.]

[19: July 1, 1849. Corr., p. 170 (Amer. Hist. Assoc., Annual Report, 1911, vol. II.).]

[20: Johnston, Stephens, pp. 238-239, 244; Smith, Political History of Slavery, 1. 121.]

[21: Laws (Ga.), 1850, pp. 122, 405-410.]

[22: Johnston, Stephens, p. 247.]

[23: Corr., pp. 184,193-195, 206-208, July 21. Newspapers, see Brooks, in Miss. Valley Hist. Review, IX. 289.]

[24: Phillips, Georgia and State Rights, pp. 163-166.]

[25: Ames, Documents, pp. 271-272; Hearon, p. 190.]

[26: 1854, Amer. Hist. Review, VIII. 92-97; 1857, Johnston, Stephens, pp. 321-322; infra, pp. 267, 268.]

[27: Hammond MSS., Jan. 27, Feb. 8; Virginia Resolves, Feb. 12; Ambler, Sectionalism in Virginia, p. 246; N. Y. Tribune, June 14; M. R. H. Garnett, Union Past and Future, published between Jan. 24 and Mar. 7. Alabama: Hodgson, Cradle of the Confederacy, p. 281; Dubose, Yancey, pp. 247-249, 481; Fleming, Civil War and Reconstruction in Alabama, p. 13; Cobb, Corr., pp. 193-195, 207. President Tyler of the College of William and Mary kindly furnished evidence of Garnett's authorship; see J. M. Garnett, in Southern Literary Messenger, I. 255.]

[28: Resolutions, Feb. 12, 1850; Acts, 1850, pp. 223-224; 1851, p. 201.]

[29: Stephens, Corr., p. 192; Globe, XXII. II. 1208.]

[30: Boston Daily Advertiser, Feb. 23.]

[31: South Carolina, Acts, 1849, p, 240, and the following Laws or Acts, all 1850: Georgia, pp. 418, 405-410, 122; Texas, pp. 93-94, 171; Tennessee, p. 572 (Globe, XXI. I. 417. Cole, Whig Party in the South, p. 161); Mississippi, pp. 526-528; Virginia, p. 233; Alabama, Weekly Tribune, Feb. 23, Daily, Feb. 25.]

[32: White, Miss. Valley Hist. Assoc., III. 283.]

[33: Senate Miscellaneous, 1849-1850, no. 24.]

[34: Hamer, p. 40; cf. Cole, Whig Party in the South, p. 162; Cong. Globe, Mar. 5.]

[35: Coleman, Crittenden, I. 333, 350.]

[36: Clayton MSS., Apr. 6; cf. Coleman, Crittenden, I. 369.]

[37: Smith, History of Slavery, 1. 121; Clay, Oct., 1851, letter, in Curtis, Webster, II, 584-585.]

[38: Clingman, and Wilmington Resolutions, Globe, XXI. I. 200-205, 311; National Intelligencer, Feb. 25; Cobb, Corr., pp. 217-218; Boyd, "North Carolina on the Eve of Secession," in Amer. Hist. Assoc., Annual Report (1910), pp. 167-177.]

[39: Hearndon, Nashville Convention, p. 283.]

[40: Johnston, Stephens, p. 247; Corr., pp. 186, 193, 194, 206-207; Hammond MSS., Jan. 27, Feb. 8.]

[41: Ames, Calhoun, p. 26.]

[42: Webster, Writings and Speeches, X. 161-162.]

[43: Cyclopedia Miss. Hist., art. "Sharkey."]

[44: Hearon, pp. 124, 171-174. Davis to Clayton (Clayton MSS.), Nov. 22, 1851.]

[45: Globe, XXI. I. 418, 124, 712; infra, p. 268.]

[46: MSS., Mar. 10. AM. HIST. REV., voL. xxvii.--18.]

[47: Anstell, Bethlehem, May 21, Greenough Collection.]

[48: Anderson, Tenn., Apr. 8, ibid.]

[49: Goode, Hunter Corr., Amer. Hist. Assoc., Annual Report (1916, vol. II.), p. 111.]

[50: Ames, Calhoun, pp. 24-27.]

[51: Hearon, pp. 120-123; Anonymous, Letter on Southern Wrongs. .. in Reply to Grayson (Charleston, 1850).]

[52: Letters, II. 111, 121, 127.]

[53: Winthrop MSS., Jan. 16, Feb. 7.]

[54: Philadelphia Bulletin, in McMaster, VIII. 15.]

[55: Winthrop MSS., Feb. 10, 6.]

[56: Writings and Speeches, XVI. 533; XVIII. 355.]

[57: Stephens, War between the States, II. 201-205, 232; Cong. Globe, XXI. I. 375-384.]

[58: Thurlow Weed, Life, II. 177-178, 180-181 (Gen. Pleasanton's confirmatory letter). Wilson, Slave Power, II. 249. Both corroborated by Hamline letter Rhodes, I. 134. Stephens's letters, N. Y. Herald, July 13, Aug, 8, 1876, denying threatening language used by Taylor "in my presence," do not nullify evidence of Taylor's attitude. Mann, Life, p. 292. Private Washington letter, Feb. 23, reporting interview, N. Y. Tribune, Feb. 25.]

[59: Weekly Tribune, Mar. 2, reprinted from Daily, Feb. 27. Cf. Washington National Intelligencer, Feb. 21, quoting: Richmond Enquirer; Wilmington Commercial; Columbia Telegraph.]

[60: New York Herald, Feb. 25; Boston Daily Advertiser, Feb. 26.]

[61: Tribune, Feb. 25.]

[62: Writings and Speeches, XVI. 534.]

[63: Lodge's reproduction of Parton, pp. 16-17, 98, 195, 325-326, 349, 353, 356, 360. Other errors in Lodge's Webster, pp. 45, 314, 322, 328, 329-330, 352.]

[64: Writings and Speeches, XVIII. 356, 387; XVI. 542, W; X. 116; Curtis, Life II. 596; XIII. 434.]

[65: Mar. 19, Cong. Globe, XXII. II. 1063.]

[66: Aug. 12, ibid., p. 1562.]

[67: U. S. Bonds (1867). About 112-113, Dec., Jan., Feb., 1850; "inactive" before Webster's speech; "firmer," Mar. 8; advanced to 117, 119, May; 116-117 after Compromise.]

[68: E. P. Wheeler, Sixty Years of American Life, p. 6; cf. Webster's Buffalo Speech, Curtis, Life, II. 576; Weed, Autobiography, p. 596.]

[69: Winthrop MSS.]

[69¹: Writings and Speeches, XVI. 534-5.]

[70: Webster to Harvey, Apr. 7, MS. Middletown (Conn.) Hist. Soc., adds Fletcher's name. Received through the kindness of Professor George M. Dutcher.]

[71: Writings and Speeches, X. 57; "Notes for the Speech," 281-291; Winthrop MSS., Apr. 3.]

[72: Writings and Speeches, XVIII. 371-372.]

[73: Blaine, Twenty Years of Congress, I. 269-271.]

[74: Works, II. 202-203.]

[75: Writings and Speeches, XVI. 580-581.]

[76: Seward, Works, III. 111-116.]
[77: Writings and Speeches, X. 57, 97.]
[78: Ibid., XIII. 595; X. 65.]
[781: Garrison childishly printed Eliot's name upside down, and between black lines, Liberator, Sept. 20.]
[79: Mar. 10. MS., "Private," to Governor Clifford.]
[80: Mar 11, Apr. 13. Webster papers, N.H. Hist. Soc., cited hereafter as "N.H.".]
[81: Mar. 11, 25, 22, 17, 26, 28, Greenough Collection, hereafter as "Greenough."]
[82: May 20. N.H.]
[83: Apr. 19, May 4. N.H.]
[84: Apr. 1. Greenough.]
[85: Writings and Speeches, XVIII. 357.]
[86: Apr. 19. N.H.]
[87: June 12. N.H.]
[88: Dec. 13. N.H.]
[89: Writings and SPeeches, XVI. 582.]
[90: Winthrop MSS., Mar. 21 and Apr. 10, 1850, Nov. 1951; Curtis, Life, II. 580; Everett's Memoir; Webster's Works (1851), I. clvii.]
[93: Barnard, Albany, Apr. 19. N.H.]
[94: Mar. 15, 28. N.H.]
[95: June 10. Greenough.]
[96: Mar. 28. Greenough.]
[97: H. L Anderson, Tenn., Apr. 8. Greenough.]
[98: Nelson, Va., May 2. N.H.]
[99: Mar. 8. Greenough.]
[100: Pp. 17-20.]
[101: August, 1850; 127 signatures. N.H.]
[102: Ogg, Webster, p. 379; Rhodes, I. 157-58.]
[103: New York Journal of Commerce, Boston Advertiser, Richmond Whig Mar. 12; Baltimore Sun, Mar. 18; Ames, Calhoun, p. 25; Boston Watchman and Reflector, in Liberator, Apr. 1.]
[104: War between the States, II. 211.]

[105: War of the Rebellion (1866), pp. 130-131.]

[106: Slave Power, II. 246.]

[107: Scribner's Magazine XXVI. 84.]

[108: Garrison, Westward Expansion, pp. 327-332; Chadwick, The Causes of the Civil War, pp. 49-51; Smith, Parties and Slavery, p. 9; Merriam, Life of Bowles, I. 81.]

[109: Rhodes, I. 157, 161.]

[110: Preliminary Report, Eighth Census, 1860; Chadwick, Causes of the Civil War, p. 28.]

[111: Oct. 2, 1950. Writings and Speeches, XVI. 568-569.]

[112: Scribner, XXVI. 84; American Law Review, XXXV. 804.]

[113: Nicolay and Hay, IX. 76.]

www.bookjungle.com *email: sales@bookjungle.com fax: 630-214-0564 mail: Book Jungle PO Box 2226 Champaign, IL 61825*

The Codes Of Hammurabi And Moses
W. W. Davies

QTY

The discovery of the Hammurabi Code is one of the greatest achievements of archaeology, and is of paramount interest, not only to the student of the Bible, but also to all those interested in ancient history...

Religion   **ISBN:** *1-59462-338-4*   *Pages:*132
MSRP $12.95

The Theory of Moral Sentiments
Adam Smith

QTY

This work from 1749. contains original theories of conscience amd moral judgment and it is the foundation for systemof morals.

Philosophy   **ISBN:** *1-59462-777-0*   *Pages:*536
MSRP $19.95

Jessica's First Prayer
Hesba Stretton

QTY

In a screened and secluded corner of one of the many railway-bridges which span the streets of London there could be seen a few years ago, from five o'clock every morning until half past eight, a tidily set-out coffee-stall, consisting of a trestle and board, upon which stood two large tin cans, with a small fire of charcoal burning under each so as to keep the coffee boiling during the early hours of the morning when the work-people were thronging into the city on their way to their daily toil...

Childrens   **ISBN:** *1-59462-373-2*   *Pages:*84
MSRP $9.95

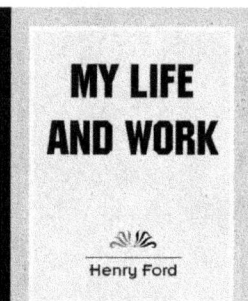

My Life and Work
Henry Ford

QTY

Henry Ford revolutionized the world with his implementation of mass production for the Model T automobile. Gain valuable business insight into his life and work with his own auto-biography... "We have only started on our development of our country we have not as yet, with all our talk of wonderful progress, done more than scratch the surface. The progress has been wonderful enough but..."

Biographies/   **ISBN:** *1-59462-198-5*   *Pages:*300
MSRP $21.95

www.bookjungle.com email: sales@bookjungle.com fax: 630-214-0564 mail: Book Jungle PO Box 2226 Champaign, IL 61825

The Art of Cross-Examination
Francis Wellman

QTY

I presume it is the experience of every author, after his first book is published upon an important subject, to be almost overwhelmed with a wealth of ideas and illustrations which could readily have been included in his book, and which to his own mind, at least, seem to make a second edition inevitable. Such certainly was the case with me; and when the first edition had reached its sixth impression in five months, I rejoiced to learn that it seemed to my publishers that the book had met with a sufficiently favorable reception to justify a second and considerably enlarged edition. ..

Reference   ISBN: *1-59462-647-2*   Pages:412   MSRP *$19.95*

On the Duty of Civil Disobedience
Henry David Thoreau

QTY

Thoreau wrote his famous essay, On the Duty of Civil Disobedience, as a protest against an unjust but popular war and the immoral but popular institution of slave-owning. He did more than write—he declined to pay his taxes, and was hauled off to gaol in consequence. Who can say how much this refusal of his hastened the end of the war and of slavery ?

Law   ISBN: *1-59462-747-9*   Pages:48   MSRP *$7.45*

Dream Psychology Psychoanalysis for Beginners
Sigmund Freud

QTY

Sigmund Freud, born Sigismund Schlomo Freud (May 6, 1856 - September 23, 1939), was a Jewish-Austrian neurologist and psychiatrist who co-founded the psychoanalytic school of psychology. Freud is best known for his theories of the unconscious mind, especially involving the mechanism of repression; his redefinition of sexual desire as mobile and directed towards a wide variety of objects; and his therapeutic techniques, especially his understanding of transference in the therapeutic relationship and the presumed value of dreams as sources of insight into unconscious desires.

Psychology   ISBN: *1-59462-905-6*   Pages:196   MSRP *$15.45*

The Miracle of Right Thought
Orison Swett Marden

QTY

Believe with all of your heart that you will do what you were made to do. When the mind has once formed the habit of holding cheerful, happy, prosperous pictures, it will not be easy to form the opposite habit. It does not matter how improbable or how far away this realization may see, or how dark the prospects may be, if we visualize them as best we can, as vividly as possible, hold tenaciously to them and vigorously struggle to attain them, they will gradually become actualized, realized in the life. But a desire, a longing without endeavor, a yearning abandoned or held indifferently will vanish without realization.

Self Help   ISBN: *1-59462-644-8*   Pages:360   MSRP *$25.45*

www.bookjungle.com *email: sales@bookjungle.com fax: 630-214-0564 mail: Book Jungle PO Box 2226 Champaign, IL 61825*

QTY

	Title	ISBN	Price
☐	**The Rosicrucian Cosmo-Conception Mystic Christianity** by *Max Heindel*	ISBN: *1-59462-188-8*	**$38.95**

The Rosicrucian Cosmo-conception is not dogmatic, neither does it appeal to any other authority than the reason of the student. It is: not controversial, but is: sent forth in the, hope that it may help to clear...
New Age/Religion Pages 646

☐ **Abandonment To Divine Providence** by *Jean-Pierre de Caussade* ISBN: *1-59462-228-0* **$25.95**
"The Rev. Jean Pierre de Caussade was one of the most remarkable spiritual writers of the Society of Jesus in France in the 18th Century. His death took place at Toulouse in 1751. His works have gone through many editions and have been republished...
Inspirational/Religion Pages 400

☐ **Mental Chemistry** by *Charles Haanel* ISBN: *1-59462-192-6* **$23.95**
Mental Chemistry allows the change of material conditions by combining and appropriately utilizing the power of the mind. Much like applied chemistry creates something new and unique out of careful combinations of chemicals the mastery of mental chemistry...
New Age Pages 354

☐ **The Letters of Robert Browning and Elizabeth Barret Barrett 1845-1846 vol II** ISBN: *1-59462-193-4* **$35.95**
by *Robert Browning* and *Elizabeth Barrett*
Biographies Pages 596

☐ **Gleanings In Genesis (volume I)** by *Arthur W. Pink* ISBN: *1-59462-130-6* **$27.45**
Appropriately has Genesis been termed "the seed plot of the Bible" for in it we have, in germ form, almost all of the great doctrines which are afterwards fully developed in the books of Scripture which follow...
Religion/Inspirational Pages 420

☐ **The Master Key** by *L. W. de Laurence* ISBN: *1-59462-001-6* **$30.95**
In no branch of human knowledge has there been a more lively increase of the spirit of research during the past few years than in the study of Psychology, Concentration and Mental Discipline. The requests for authentic lessons in Thought Control, Mental Discipline and... *New Age/Business Pages 422*

☐ **The Lesser Key Of Solomon Goetia** by *L. W. de Laurence* ISBN: *1-59462-092-X* **$9.95**
This translation of the first book of the "Lernegton" which is now for the first time made accessible to students of Talismanic Magic was done, after careful collation and edition, from numerous Ancient Manuscripts in Hebrew, Latin, and French...
New Age/Occult Pages 92

☐ **Rubaiyat Of Omar Khayyam** by *Edward Fitzgerald* ISBN: *1-59462-332-5* **$13.95**
Edward Fitzgerald, whom the world has already learned, in spite of his own efforts to remain within the shadow of anonymity, to look upon as one of the rarest poets of the century, was born at Bredfield, in Suffolk, on the 31st of March, 1809. He was the third son of John Purcell... *Music Pages 172*

☐ **Ancient Law** by *Henry Maine* ISBN: *1-59462-128-4* **$29.95**
The chief object of the following pages is to indicate some of the earliest ideas of mankind, as they are reflected in Ancient Law, and to point out the relation of those ideas to modern thought.
Religion/History Pages 452

☐ **Far-Away Stories** by *William J. Locke* ISBN: *1-59462-129-2* **$19.45**
"Good wine needs no bush, but a collection of mixed vintages does. And this book is just such a collection. Some of the stories I do not want to remain buried for ever in the museum files of dead magazine-numbers an author's not unpardonable vanity..."
Fiction Pages 272

☐ **Life of David Crockett** by *David Crockett* ISBN: *1-59462-250-7* **$27.45**
"Colonel David Crockett was one of the most remarkable men of the times in which he lived. Born in humble life, but gifted with a strong will, an indomitable courage, and unremitting perseverance...
Biographies/New Age Pages 424

☐ **Lip-Reading** by *Edward Nitchie* ISBN: *1-59462-206-X* **$25.95**
Edward B. Nitchie, founder of the New York School for the Hard of Hearing, now the Nitchie School of Lip-Reading, Inc, wrote "LIP-READING Principles and Practice". The development and perfecting of this meritorious work on lip-reading was an undertaking... *How-to Pages 400*

☐ **A Handbook of Suggestive Therapeutics, Applied Hypnotism, Psychic Science** ISBN: *1-59462-214-0* **$24.95**
by *Henry Munro*
Health/New Age/Health/Self-help Pages 376

☐ **A Doll's House: and Two Other Plays** by *Henrik Ibsen* ISBN: *1-59462-112-8* **$19.95**
Henrik Ibsen created this classic when in revolutionary 1848 Rome. Introducing some striking concepts in playwriting for the realist genre, this play has been studied the world over.
Fiction/Classics/Plays 308

☐ **The Light of Asia** by *sir Edwin Arnold* ISBN: *1-59462-204-3* **$13.95**
In this poetic masterpiece, Edwin Arnold describes the life and teachings of Buddha. The man who was to become known as Buddha to the world was born as Prince Gautama of India but he rejected the worldly riches and abandoned the reigns of power when... *Religion/History/Biographies Pages 170*

☐ **The Complete Works of Guy de Maupassant** by *Guy de Maupassant* ISBN: *1-59462-157-8* **$16.95**
"For days and days, nights and nights, I had dreamed of that first kiss which was to consecrate our engagement, and I knew not on what spot I should put my lips..."
Fiction/Classics Pages 240

☐ **The Art of Cross-Examination** by *Francis L. Wellman* ISBN: *1-59462-309-0* **$26.95**
Written by a renowned trial lawyer, Wellman imparts his experience and uses case studies to explain how to use psychology to extract desired information through questioning.
How-to/Science/Reference Pages 408

☐ **Answered or Unanswered?** by *Louisa Vaughan* ISBN: *1-59462-248-5* **$10.95**
Miracles of Faith in China
Religion Pages 112

☐ **The Edinburgh Lectures on Mental Science (1909)** by *Thomas* ISBN: *1-59462-008-3* **$11.95**
This book contains the substance of a course of lectures recently given by the writer in the Queen Street Hall, Edinburgh. Its purpose is to indicate the Natural Principles governing the relation between Mental Action and Material Conditions...
New Age/Psychology Pages 148

☐ **Ayesha** by *H. Rider Haggard* ISBN: *1-59462-301-5* **$24.95**
Verily and indeed it is the unexpected that happens! Probably if there was one person upon the earth from whom the Editor of this, and of a certain previous history, did not expect to hear again...
Classics Pages 380

☐ **Ayala's Angel** by *Anthony Trollope* ISBN: *1-59462-352-X* **$29.95**
The two girls were both pretty, but Lucy who was twenty-one who supposed to be simple and comparatively unattractive, whereas Ayala was credited, as her Bombwhat romantic name might show, with poetic charm and a taste for romance. Ayala when her father died was nineteen... *Fiction Pages 484*

☐ **The American Commonwealth** by *James Bryce* ISBN: *1-59462-286-8* **$34.45**
An interpretation of American democratic political theory. It examines political mechanics and society from the perspective of Scotsman James Bryce
Politics Pages 572

☐ **Stories of the Pilgrims** by *Margaret P. Pumphrey* ISBN: *1-59462-116-0* **$17.95**
This book explores pilgrims religious oppression in England as well as their escape to Holland and eventual crossing to America on the Mayflower, and their early days in New England...
History Pages 268

www.bookjungle.com *email: sales@bookjungle.com fax: 630-214-0564 mail: Book Jungle PO Box 2226 Champaign, IL 61825*

			QTY
The Fasting Cure *by Sinclair Upton*	ISBN: *1-59462-222-1*	**$13.95**	
In the Cosmopolitan Magazine for May, 1910, and in the Contemporary Review (London) for April, 1910, I published an article dealing with my experiences in fasting. I have written a great many magazine articles, but never one which attracted so much attention...		*New Age/Self Help/Health Pages 164*	
Hebrew Astrology *by Sepharial*	ISBN: *1-59462-308-2*	**$13.45**	
In these days of advanced thinking it is a matter of common observation that we have left many of the old landmarks behind and that we are now pressing forward to greater heights and to a wider horizon than that which represented the mind-content of our progenitors...		*Astrology Pages 144*	
Thought Vibration or The Law of Attraction in the Thought World	ISBN: *1-59462-127-6*	**$12.95**	
by William Walker Atkinson		*Psychology/Religion Pages 144*	
Optimism *by Helen Keller*	ISBN: *1-59462-108-X*	**$15.95**	
Helen Keller was blind, deaf, and mute since 19 months old, yet famously learned how to overcome these handicaps, communicate with the world, and spread her lectures promoting optimism. An inspiring read for everyone...		*Biographies/Inspirational Pages 84*	
Sara Crewe *by Frances Burnett*	ISBN: *1-59462-360-0*	**$9.45**	
In the first place, Miss Minchin lived in London. Her home was a large, dull, tall one, in a large, dull square, where all the houses were alike, and all the sparrows were alike, and where all the door-knockers made the same heavy sound...		*Childrens/Classic Pages 88*	
The Autobiography of Benjamin Franklin *by Benjamin Franklin*	ISBN: *1-59462-135-7*	**$24.95**	
The Autobiography of Benjamin Franklin has probably been more extensively read than any other American historical work, and no other book of its kind has had such ups and downs of fortune. Franklin lived for many years in England, where he was agent...		*Biographies/History Pages 332*	

Name	
Email	
Telephone	
Address	
City, State ZIP	

☐ Credit Card   ☐ Check / Money Order

Credit Card Number	
Expiration Date	
Signature	

Please Mail to: Book Jungle
PO Box 2226
Champaign, IL 61825
or Fax to: 630-214-0564

ORDERING INFORMATION

web: *www.bookjungle.com*
email: *sales@bookjungle.com*
fax: *630-214-0564*
mail: *Book Jungle PO Box 2226 Champaign, IL 61825*
or PayPal *to sales@bookjungle.com*

Please contact us for bulk discounts

DIRECT-ORDER TERMS

20% Discount if You Order Two or More Books
Free Domestic Shipping!
Accepted: Master Card, Visa, Discover, American Express

www.ingramcontent.com/pod-product-compliance
Lightning Source LLC
Chambersburg PA
CBHW081331040426

42453CB00013B/2377